27 Star Patchwork Patterns
with Plastic Templates

Rita Weiss

DOVER PUBLICATIONS, INC.
New York

Bibliographical Note

27 Star Patchwork Patterns with Plastic Templates is an unabridged, retitled (1993) reprint of the work first published as *Plastic Templates for 27 Star Patchwork Patterns* by Dover Publications, Inc., in 1988.

Library of Congress Cataloging-in-Publication Data

Weiss, Rita.
    27 star patchwork patterns with plastic templates / by Rita Weiss.
        p.   cm.
    ISBN 0-486-25844-0 (pbk.)
    1. Quilting—Patterns. 2. Patchwork—Patterns. I. Title. II. Title: Plastic templates for twenty-seven star patchwork patterns. III. Title: Star patchwork patterns.
TT835.W453 1988
746.9′7041—dc19   88-23737
                                                   CIP

Manufactured in the United States of America
Dover Publications, Inc., 31 East 2nd Street, Mineola, N.Y. 11501

Introduction

Among the most popular of quilt patterns are those that are star designs. The 27 quilt patterns in this book are all based on the 8-pointed star.

The blocks are all the same size and therefore can be used together to create sampler quilts, or one block can be repeated over and over again to give you an entire quilt made of one design. Many of these blocks create wonderful optical illusions when an entire quilt is made of the same block. If you prefer, you can repeat two or three different blocks in one quilt. The number of quilts you can make with this one book, therefore, is almost endless.

The special feature of this book is the plastic templates located in an envelope attached to the inside back cover of the book. Every quilt in this collection can be made with these templates. No more scaling up of blocks; no more tracing patterns; no more gluing designs onto sandpaper or cardboard. These templates are ready to be used the moment that they are cut out. Best of all, they can be used over and over again to create a multitude of quilts!

In most cases, colors have not been specified for the quilt blocks; instead we have indicated light, bright, medium, dark and very dark fabrics. For two of the blocks, however, the Christmas Star and the Patriotic Star, we do suggest colors. In general, you should feel free to use your own color scheme, making your blocks more or less complicated and more or less subtle in order to achieve quilts that are your personal creations.

As the title indicates, this work is a collection of immediately usable patterns—not an instruction book on how to do patchwork; that subject is already well covered in numerous inexpensive books, and limitations of space permit us only to sketch out the process in brief.

BEGINNING THE QUILT

Before cutting out the pieces for an entire quilt, always make one block of the pattern. This gives you a chance to double-check your pattern and to make certain that you like both the pattern and the color choices.

Kinds of Materials

Old-time quilts were traditionally made with 100% cotton, and this is still the fabric most experienced quilt makers prefer. If you want to use a blend, try not to use anything that has more than 30% synthetic fiber.

Before you begin to work on your quilt, be sure to wash your fabric to check that it is colorfast and pre-shrunk. Fabrics that continue to bleed after they have been washed should be eliminated.

Press all fabric to remove wrinkles and crease marks. Check the grain line of the fabric carefully. Lengthwise threads should be parallel to the selvage and crosswise threads should be perpendicular to insure that the pieces will be correctly cut.

The amount of fabric you will need for an entire quilt of each block is given with the instructions for making that block. The requirements we give are generous, but not so generous that you can waste fabric. If you are able to cut your pieces by sharing a common cutting line, as shown below, you will need less fabric than we indicate. If you leave

a great deal of space between pieces, you may be in danger of running out of fabric. All fabric requirements are based on 44"–45" fabric. If you use other widths, you must adjust accordingly.

Cutting the Templates

All the pattern pieces used in making these quilts are given in actual-size templates printed on special template plastic and are located in the envelope attached to the inside back cover of this book.

These templates are designed to be used for either machine or hand piecing. If you are planning to piece your blocks by machine, cut out the templates on the *solid* line, to include the ¼" seam allowance. If you are planning to piece your block by hand, cut out the templates on the broken line.

It is important that all templates be cut out carefully because if they are not accurate, the patchwork pieces will not fit together. Use a pair of good-size sharp scissors (not the scissors that you will use to cut your fabric, of course), a single-edged razor blade or an X-ACTO knife. Be careful not to round the corners of triangles.

Cutting the Pieces

Cutting the pieces is one of the most important steps in making a patchwork block. You must be accurate in order to have the pattern fit smoothly. Start by laying your laundered, freshly ironed fabric on a smooth surface, wrong side up. Have all your supplies ready: scissors, rulers, sharp pencils, templates, etc.

Cutting the Pieces for Machine Sewing. Lay the plastic template (cut on the solid lines) on the wrong side of the fabric near the top edge of the material (but not on the selvage), with one straight edge parallel to the lengthwise grain of the fabric.

Trace around the plastic. (A word of caution: always test any marking materials to make certain they will not run when wet!) Continue moving the template and tracing it on the fabric the required number of times, moving from left to right and always keeping the straight sides parallel to the grain. You will save fabric if you have the pieces share a common cutting line, but if this is confusing leave a narrow border or margin around each piece.

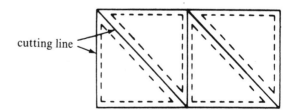

cutting line

The solid line is the cutting line. The broken line is the seam line; match to the line on the next patch. Sewing is done on the broken line. The pieces can share a common cutting line.

Cutting the Pieces for Hand Sewing. Lay the plastic template (cut on the broken lines) on the fabric as described above for machine piecing and trace around it with your marking tool.

Now measure ¼″ around this shape. Using a ruler, draw this second line. This is the line you will cut on. Notice that the first line (where you traced your template) is there to use as a guide for stitching. The seam allowance does not have to be perfect because it will not show. The sewing line, however, must be perfectly straight or the pieces will not fit together properly.

Sewing the Block

Before beginning to sew a block, lay out all the pieces that will be needed for that block. Always work with well-ironed fabric; all pieces should be ironed before they are sewn together.

Sewing the Block by Hand. Place two pieces with right sides facing, and place a pin through both pieces at each end of the pencil line. Check on the back to make sure that the pins are

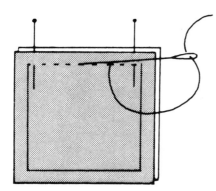

Place a pin through both pieces at each end of the pencil line.

exactly on the pencil lines. When sewing larger seams, place pins every 1½″, removing the pins as you sew past them. Always stitch on the sewing line, being careful not to stitch into the margins at the corners. Use a fairly short needle and

Do not stitch into the margins at the corners.

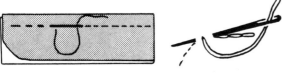

Running stitch   Backstitch

no more than an 18″ length of thread. Join the pieces with short running stitches, taking a few backstitches, rather than a knot, at the beginning and end of a seam. When you sew two bias edges together (as in sewing two triangles along the long side), try to keep the thread taut enough so that the edges do not stretch as you sew them.

After you join two pieces together, press the seams flat to one side, not open. Open seams can weaken the quilt. Generally seams can all be pressed in the same direction, but darker pieces should not be pressed so that they fall under the lighter pieces, since they may show through when the quilt is completed. All seams should be ironed before they are crossed with another seam.

Sewing the Block by Sewing Machine. Place the two pieces together with right sides facing. Pieces that are to be machine stitched should be carefully placed so that the top edges of both pieces are even. Machine piecing is best done with the straight stitch foot and throat plate on the machine. Measure ¼″ from the needle hole to the right side of the presser foot and place a piece of tape on the plate. Keep the edge of your piece lined up with this marking, and you will be able to sew with a perfect ¼″ seam line. Follow the directions for sewing the pieces together by hand; pin the seam, baste (if desired) and sew. Be careful that you do not sew over pins even if your machine permits this. Sewing over pins tends to weaken the seam. After you have joined the pieces, press the seams as described for hand sewing.

Blocking the Quilt

The term "blocking" means keeping the edges straight on all sides of the quilt so that it will be a perfect rectangle when finished. The term applies to the quilt's divisions as well as to the entire quilt, so the process of blocking is a continuous process from start to finish.

Right at the start it will help the blocking process if you have cut all of your pieces with the straight sides of the pattern parallel to the grain of the fabric, because pieces cut on the bias have a tendency to pucker.

When you have completed a block, it must be blocked before it is joined to another block. Pull the edges of the block straight with the fingers and pin the corners to the ironing board to hold them rigidly in place. Cover the block with a damp cloth and steam with a warm iron. Do not let the pressing cloth get dry. Iron the block perfectly flat with no puckers. Do the edges first and the center last. Move the iron as little as possible to keep the block from stretching. All of our blocks should be a perfect 16½″ square; the extra ¼″ all around is the seam allowance that will be used when joining the blocks.

After the quilt is set together it will need a final blocking before it is ready to be quilted.

Setting the Quilt

After you have pieced and blocked the required number of blocks, lay them out to get the final effect before setting them together. Check to see that each block is turned the proper way.

Join the blocks to make six rows of five blocks each. Use the ¼″ seam allowance at all times, and press the seams to one side. Be extremely careful that all blocks are turned in the right direction. When horizontal rows are completed, join two rows together, matching seam lines. Then add the next rows and press the seams to one side.

Adding the Border

When all of the blocks have been joined, add the border strips. Right sides together, attach one long strip to the right side of the quilt and one to the left. In the same manner sew the shorter border strips to the top and bottom. Use the ¼″ seam allowance at all times.

FINISHING THE QUILT

A completed quilt consists of three parts: the patchwork top, the filler or batting and the backing. The quilting stitches are used to lock the patchwork top firmly to both the backing and the batting in the middle.

Before you join the quilt top to the batting and backing, you will need to mark the quilting pattern on the quilt top. (A good quilting pattern is to quilt around the patchwork pieces ¼" from the seam line.) Patterns for quilting are available from many sources. A good selection of these patterns appears in *Quilting Patterns* by Linda Macho (Dover 0-486-24632-9), *Amish Quilting Patterns* by Gwen Marston and Joe Cunningham (Dover 0-486-25326-0) and *70 Classic Quilting Patterns,* also by Gwen Marston and Joe Cunningham (Dover 0-486-25474-7).

Mark all quilting lines on the *right* side of the fabric. For marking, use a hard lead pencil, chalk or one of the special water-soluble marking pens. If you quilt right on marked lines, they will not show. Be sure to test any marking material to find one that works well for you.

Quilt Backing and Batting

You should choose the backing and batting for your quilt with the greatest care if you want your quilt to endure for years. It is false economy to use inferior materials; all of your time and painstaking stitches deserve the best!

There are a number of different kinds of batting on the market. Buy a medium-weight bonded polyester sheet batting for most quilts. Don't buy polyester *stuffing,* which is intended for pillows or toys. Sheet batting is made especially for quilts; it is bonded into a flat sheet and then rolled for ease in handling.

Fabric for the backing should be soft and loosely woven so that the quilting needle can pass through evenly. Your quilt is probably wider than most available fabric so you will have to sew lengths together to make your quilt backing. When joining fabric, don't have a seam going down the center. Cut off selvages and make a center strip that is about 36" wide; have narrower strips at the sides. Seam pieces together and iron the seam open. This is the only time in making a quilt that a seam should be pressed open.

Cut the backing and batting approximately 2" wider on all sides than the quilt top. Place the backing, wrong side up, on a flat surface. Place the batting on top of this, matching the outer edges. Pin the backing and batting together; then baste with long stitches, starting in the center and sewing toward the edges in a number of diagonal lines. Now center the quilt

top, right side up, on top of the batting. Baste the top to the batting and backing layers in the same manner.

Quilting the Top

The actual quilting stitch is a simple process for anyone who can do any other form of needlework, but it does take a little practice. It is sometimes helpful to use a practice piece of two squares of material with a layer of batting in between. The stitch is just a very simple running stitch, but working through three layers at once may be a bit difficult at first.

Use one of the short, fine needles especially designed for quilting (they are called "betweens") and a 100% cotton quilting thread.

Every quilter wears a thimble! It is worn on the middle finger of your right hand (or your left, if you are left-handed). The thimble is used to push the needle through the fabric.

The quilting can be done in a traditional floor frame, but most quilting today is done in a quilting hoop. Place the hoop over the middle of the quilt; pull the quilt slightly taut (not stretched as tightly as for embroidery) and move extra fullness toward the edges. Begin working in the center and quilt toward the outer edges. As you work, you will find that the quilting stitch has a tendency to push the batting, and by working from the center out you can gradually ease any excess fullness toward the edges. If you wish, run the quilting thread through beeswax to keep it from tangling.

Begin with an 18" length of thread with a knot in one end. Go into the quilt through the top about ½" from where you plan to begin quilting, and bring the needle up on the quilting line. Pull gently but firmly and the knot will slip through the fabric into the batting, where it will disappear. Now place the left hand under the hoop where the needle should come through. With the right hand push the needle vertically downward through the layers of the quilt until it touches the left hand. As you become proficient at quilting, you'll be able to do the whole operation with one hand, merely using the left hand to signal that the needle has penetrated three layers. Experienced quilters are able to put several stitches on the needle just as if they were sewing.

Make the stitches as close together as you can; this is the real secret of beautiful quilting. The stitches should be evenly spaced, and the same length on the front as on the back. When the entire quilt has been quilted, lift it from the frame or hoop and remove the basting stitches.

Binding the Quilt

Place the quilt on a flat surface and carefully trim the backing and batting ½" beyond the edge of the quilt top. Measure the quilt top and, from the fabric used for the border, cut two 2"-wide binding strips the length of your quilt (for the sides). Right sides together, sew one side strip to one side of the quilt with a ¼" seam allowance (seam allowance should be measured from the outer edge of the quilt top fabric, not the outer edge of the batting/backing). Turn the binding to the back over the edge of the batting and the backing and turn under ¼" on the raw edge. Slip-stitch to the backing. Do the other side in the same manner. Then carefully measure the top and bottom of the quilt and cut two 2"-wide binding strips this length plus ½" for seam allowances. Attach in the same manner as for the sides, turning in seam allowances at ends.

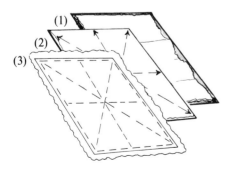

Finishing the quilt. (1) Placing batting on lining. (2) Basting batting to lining. (3) Basting marked top to batting and lining, through center and around edges.

Arabian Star

Use this 16″ block in a sampler quilt, or make 30 blocks and set them five across and six down with a 3″ border made of the bright fabric, to create an 86″ × 102″ quilt top.

Fabric requirements for quilt top

Light fabric	1½ yds
Bright fabric	2½ yds
Medium fabric	3½ yds
Dark fabric	4¼ yds
Very dark fabric	3 yds

Number of pieces to be cut

		for block	for quilt top
Template A	4 light		120 light
Template B	4 bright		120 bright
Template B	4 medium		120 medium
Template B	4 dark		120 dark
Template C	8 bright		240 bright
Template C	24 medium		720 medium
Template C	32 dark		960 dark
Template C	24 very dark		720 very dark
Border strips, 3½″ × 86½″			2 bright fabric
Border strips, 3½″ × 96½″			2 bright fabric

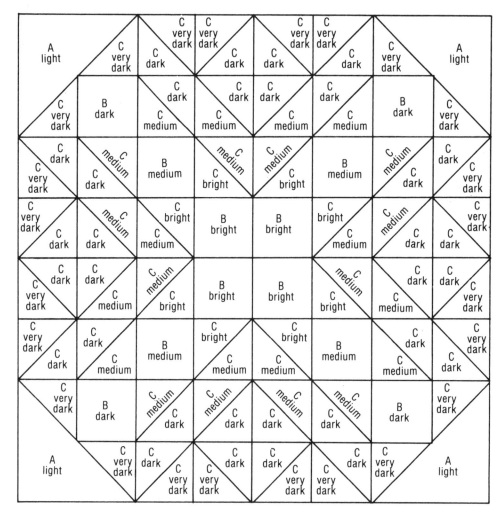

Bethlehem Star

Use this 16″ block in a sampler quilt, or make 30 blocks and set them five across and six down with a 3″ border made of the dark fabric, to create an 86″ × 102″ quilt top.

Fabric requirements for quilt top

Light fabric	3½ yds
Bright fabric	3¾ yds
Dark fabric	8 yds

Number of pieces to be cut

	for block	for quilt top
Template B	4 light	120 light
Template C	24 light	720 light
Template E	8 bright	240 bright
Template E (reversed)	8 bright	240 bright
Template E	16 dark	480 dark
Template E (reversed)	16 dark	480 dark
Border strips, 3½″ × 86½″	2 dark fabric	
Border strips, 3½″ × 96½″	2 dark fabric	

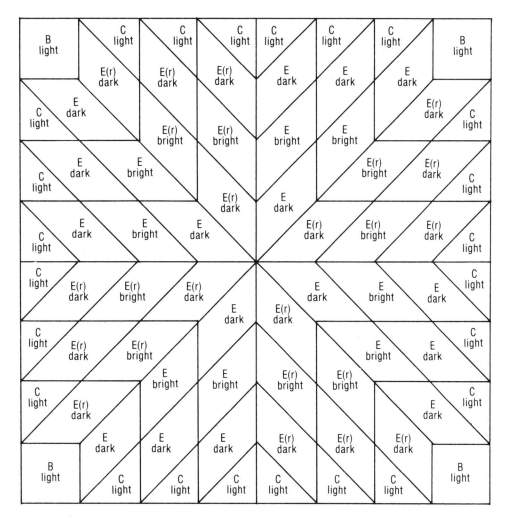

Blazing Star

Use this 16″ block in a sampler quilt, or make 30 blocks and set them five across and six down with a 3″ border made of the dark fabric, to create an 86″ × 102″ quilt top.

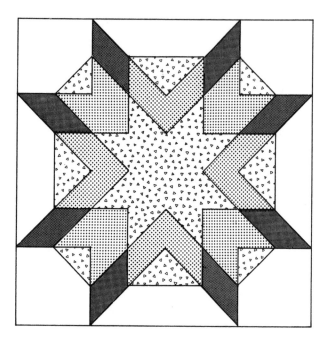

Fabric requirements for quilt top

Light fabric	5 yds
Bright fabric	3 yds
Medium fabric	3½ yds
Dark fabric	3 yds

Number of pieces to be cut

	for block	for quilt top
Template A	4 light	120 light
Template B	8 light	240 light
Template B	4 bright	120 bright
Template B	4 medium	120 medium
Template C	20 light	600 light
Template C	20 bright	600 bright
Template C	24 medium	720 medium
Template C	16 dark	480 dark
Border strips, 3½″ × 86½″		2 dark fabric
Border strips, 3½″ × 96½″		2 dark fabric

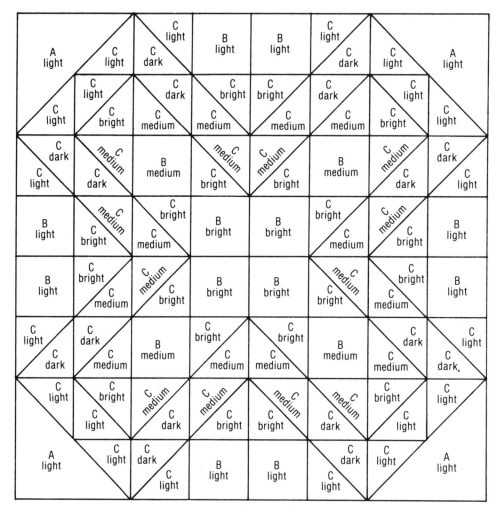

Broken Star

Use this 16″ block in a sampler quilt, or make 30 blocks and set them five across and six down with a 3″ border made of the medium fabric, to create an 86″ × 102″ quilt top.

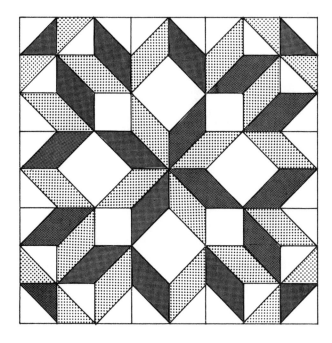

Fabric requirements for quilt top

Light fabric	5¾ yds
Medium fabric	5½ yds
Dark fabric	4¼ yds

Number of pieces to be cut

	for block	for quilt top
Template B	4 light	120 light
Template C	44 light	1320 light
Template C	8 medium	240 medium
Template C	4 dark	120 dark
Template E	12 medium	360 medium
Template E (reversed)	4 medium	120 medium
Template E	4 dark	120 dark
Template E (reversed)	12 dark	360 dark
Border strips, 3½″ × 86½″		2 medium fabric
Border strips, 3½″ × 96½″		2 medium fabric

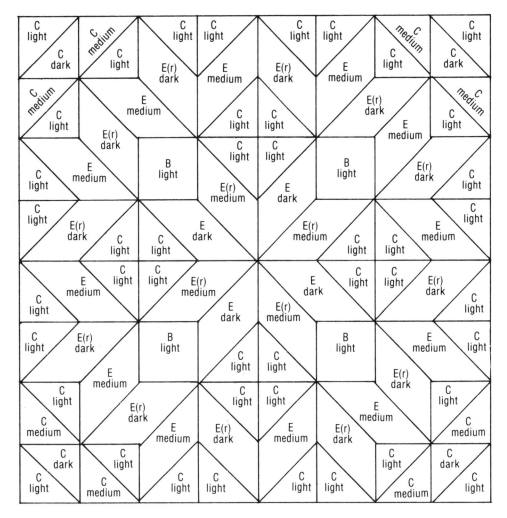

Christmas Star

Use this 16″ block in a sampler quilt, or make 30 blocks and set them five across and six down with a 3″ border made of the medium fabric, to create an 86″ × 102″ quilt top.

Fabric requirements for quilt top

Light fabric (white)	4¼ yds
Medium fabric (red)	4 yds
Dark fabric (green)	6½ yds

Number of pieces to be cut

	for block	for quilt top
Template A	4 dark	120 dark
Template B	12 dark	360 dark
Template C	36 light	1080 light
Template C	24 medium	720 medium
Template C	28 dark	840 dark
Border strips, 3½″ × 86½″	2 medium fabric	
Border strips, 3½″ × 96½″	2 medium fabric	

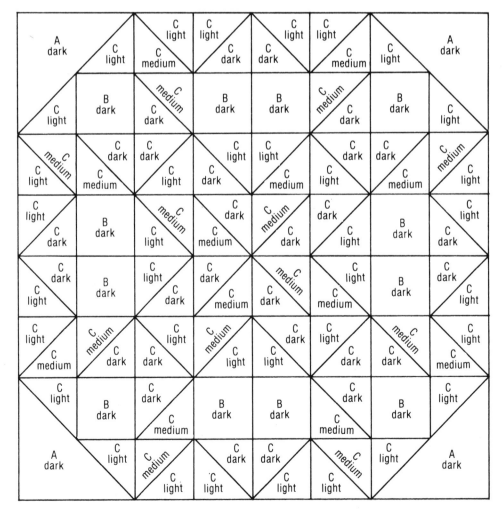

Cluster of Stars

Use this 16″ block in a sampler quilt, or make 30 blocks and set them five across and six down with a 3″ border made of the light fabric, to create an 86″ × 102″ quilt top.

Fabric requirements for quilt top

Light fabric	4¾ yds
Medium fabric	3¾ yds
Dark fabric	5¾ yds

Number of pieces to be cut

	for block	*for quilt top*
Template B	16 dark	480 dark
Template C	32 light	960 light
Template C	32 medium	960 medium
Template C	32 dark	960 dark
Border strips, 3½″ × 86½″		2 light fabric
Border strips, 3½″ × 96½″		2 light fabric

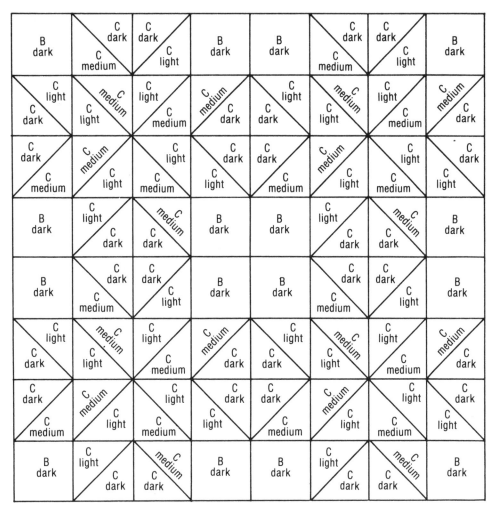

December Star

Use this 16″ block in a sampler quilt, or make 30 blocks and set them five across and six down with a 3″ border made of the bright fabric, to create an 86″ × 102″ quilt top.

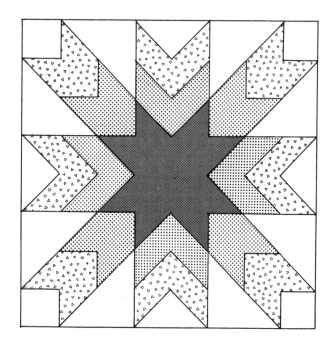

Fabric requirements for quilt top

Light fabric	4½ yds
Bright fabric	4½ yds
Medium fabric	3½ yds
Dark fabric	1½ yds

Number of pieces to be cut

		for block		for quilt top
Template B	12	light	360	light
Template B	4	bright	120	bright
Template B	4	medium	120	medium
Template B	4	dark	120	dark
Template C	24	light	720	light
Template C	24	bright	720	bright
Template C	24	medium	720	medium
Template C	8	dark	240	dark
Border strips, 3½″ × 86½″			2	bright fabric
Border strips, 3½″ × 96½″			2	bright fabric

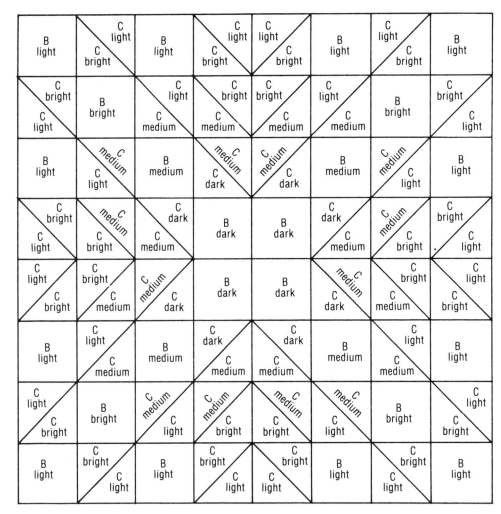

Enclosed Stars

Use this 16″ block in a sampler quilt, or make 30 blocks and set them five across and six down with a 3″ border made of the dark fabric, to create an 86″ × 102″ quilt top.

Fabric requirements for quilt top

Light fabric	7½ yds
Medium fabric	4¾ yds
Dark fabric	4 yds

Number of pieces to be cut

	for block	*for quilt top*
Template C	64 light	1920 light
Template C	40 medium	1200 medium
Template C	24 dark	720 dark
Border strips, 3½″ × 86½″		2 dark fabric
Border strips, 3½″ × 96½″		2 dark fabric

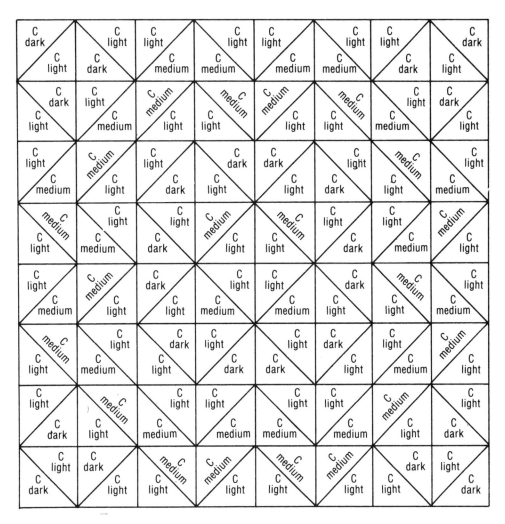

Evening Star

Use this 16″ block in a sampler quilt, or make 30 blocks and set them five across and six down with a 3″ border made of the dark fabric, to create an 86″ × 102″ quilt top.

Fabric requirements for quilt top

Light fabric	9 yds
Dark fabric	4 yds

Number of pieces to be cut

		for block	*for quilt top*
Template A	24 light	720 light	
Template A	8 dark	240 dark	
Border strips, 3½″ × 86½″			2 dark fabric
Border strips, 3½″ × 96½″			2 dark fabric

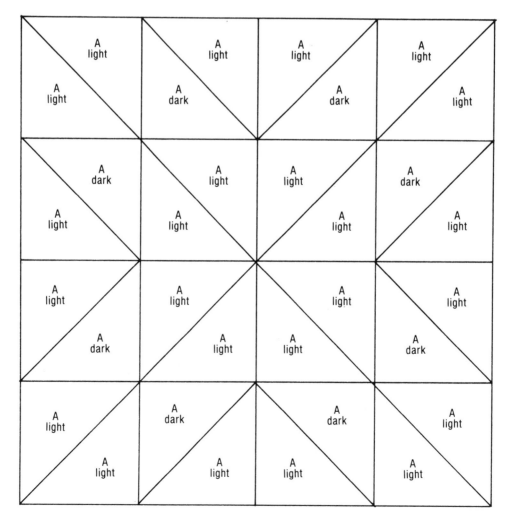

Feathered Star

Use this 16″ block in a sampler quilt, or make 30 blocks and set them five across and six down with a 3″ border made of the light fabric, to create an 86″ × 102″ quilt top.

Fabric requirements for quilt top

Light fabric	9¾ yds
Dark fabric	5½ yds

Number of pieces to be cut

	for block		*for quilt top*	
Template A	16	light	480	light
Template B	8	dark	240	dark
Template C	4	light	120	light
Template C	16	dark	480	dark
Template D	52	light	1560	light
Template D	60	dark	1800	dark
Border strips, 3½″ × 86½″			2 light fabric	
Border strips, 3½″ × 96½″			2 light fabric	

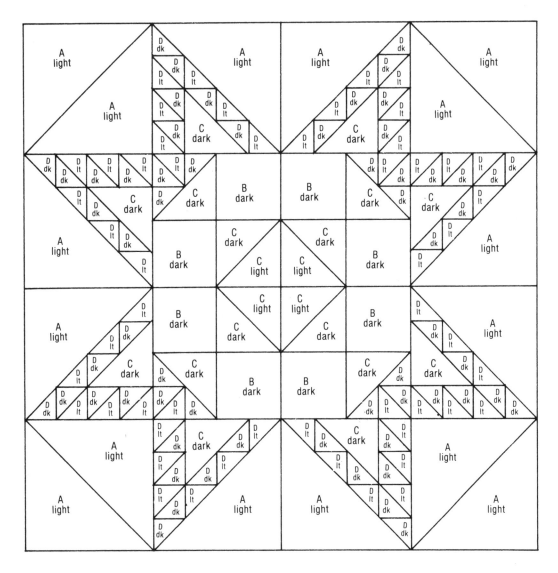

Heavenly Stars

Use this 16″ block in a sampler quilt, or make 30 blocks and set them five across and six down with a 3″ border made of the medium fabric, to create an 86″ × 102″ quilt top.

Fabric requirements for quilt top

Light fabric	3 yds
Bright fabric	5¾ yds
Medium fabric	4 yds
Dark fabric	1 yd
Very dark fabric	1 yd

Number of pieces to be cut

		for block	*for quilt top*
Template B	16 bright		480 bright
Template C	24 light		720 light
Template C	32 bright		960 bright
Template C	24 medium		720 medium
Template C	8 dark		240 dark
Template C	8 very dark		240 very dark
Border strips, 3½″ × 86½″			2 medium fabric
Border strips, 3½″ × 96½″			2 medium fabric

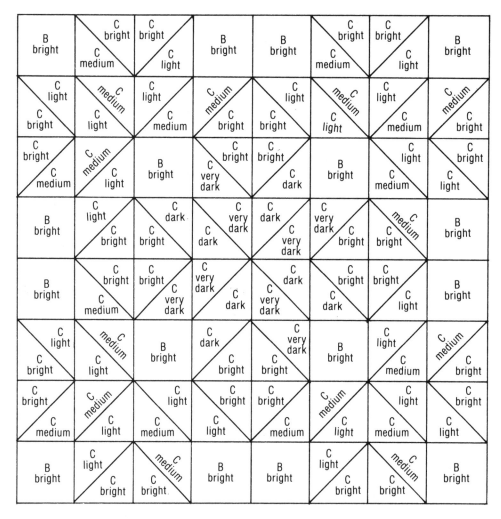

LeMoyne Star

Use this 16″ block in a sampler quilt, or make 30 blocks and set them five across and six down with a 3″ border made of the dark fabric, to create an 86″ × 102″ quilt top.

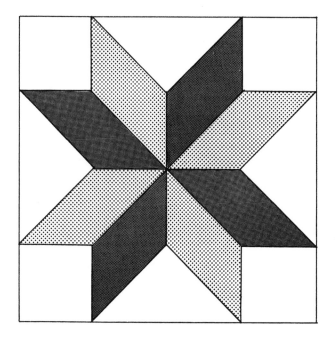

Fabric requirements for quilt top

Light fabric	6 yds
Medium fabric	3 yds
Dark fabric	4 yds

Number of pieces to be cut

	for block		for quilt top	
Template A	16	light	480	light
Template A	8	medium	240	medium
Template A	8	dark	240	dark
Border strips, 3½″ × 86½″			2	dark fabric
Border strips, 3½″ × 96½″			2	dark fabric

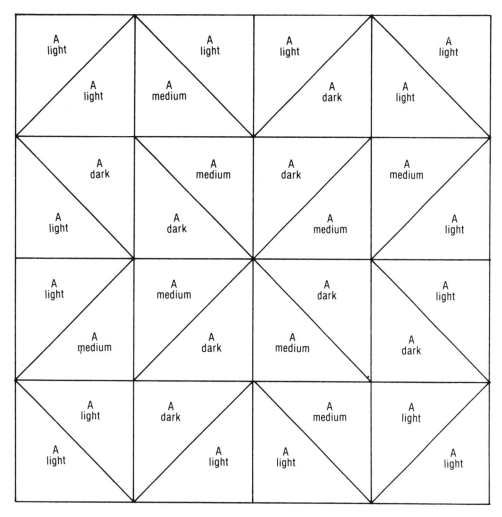

Linked Stars

Use this 16″ block in a sampler quilt, or make 30 blocks and set them five across and six down with a 3″ border made of the medium fabric, to create an 86″ × 102″ quilt top.

Fabric requirements for quilt top

Light fabric	5 yds
Bright fabric	1¼ yds
Medium fabric	2 yds
Dark fabric	3 yds

Number of pieces to be cut

		for block	*for quilt top*
Template B	24 light		720 light
Template B	8 bright		240 bright
Template B	8 medium		240 medium
Template B	8 dark		240 dark
Template C	16 light		480 light
Template C	16 dark		480 dark

Border strips, 3½″ × 86½″   2 medium fabric
Border strips, 3½″ × 96½″   2 medium fabric

Lucinda's Star

Use this 16″ block in a sampler quilt, or make 30 blocks and set them five across and six down with a 3″ border made of the dark fabric, to create an 86″ × 102″ quilt top.

Fabric requirements for quilt top

Light fabric	3 yds
Medium print fabric	3½ yds
Medium fabric	3½ yds
Dark fabric	3½ yds
Dark print fabric	3½ yds

Number of pieces to be cut

		for block		for quilt top	
Template A		4	light	120	light
Template C		12	light	360	light
Template D		84	medium	2520	medium
Template D		60	dark	1800	dark
Template E		16	dark print	480	dark print
Template E (reversed)		16	medium print	480	medium print

Border strips, 3½″ × 86½″	2	dark fabric
Border strips, 3½″ × 96½″	2	dark fabric

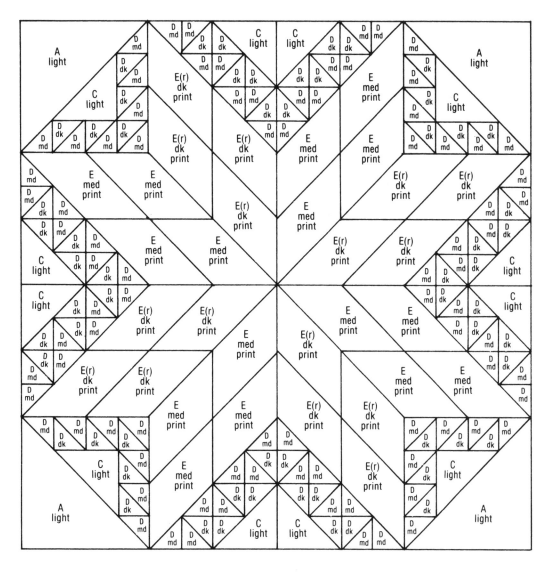

Missouri Star

Use this 16″ block in a sampler quilt, or make 30 blocks and set them five across and six down with a 3″ border made of the medium fabric, to create an 86″ × 102″ quilt top.

Fabric requirements for quilt top

Light fabric	3½ yds
Medium fabric	4½ yds
Dark fabric	6 yds

Number of pieces to be cut

		for block		*for quilt top*
Template A	4	light	120	light
Template A	4	medium	120	medium
Template A	16	dark	480	dark
Template C	16	light	480	light
Template C	16	medium	480	medium
Border strips, 3½″ × 86½″			2	medium fabric
Border strips, 3½″ × 96½″			2	medium fabric

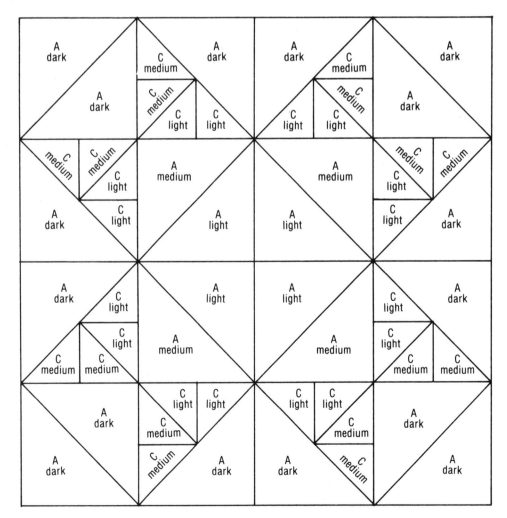

Northumberland Star

Use this 16″ block in a sampler quilt, or make 30 blocks and set them five across and six down with a 3″ border made of the dark fabric, to create an 86″ × 102″ quilt top.

Fabric requirements for quilt top

Light fabric	9 yds
Dark fabric	4¾ yds

Number of pieces to be cut

	for block	for quilt top
Template A	10 light	300 light
Template B	12 light	360 light
Template C	32 light	960 light
Template C	32 dark	960 dark
Border strips, 3½″ × 86½″		2 dark fabric
Border strips, 3½″ × 96½″		2 dark fabric

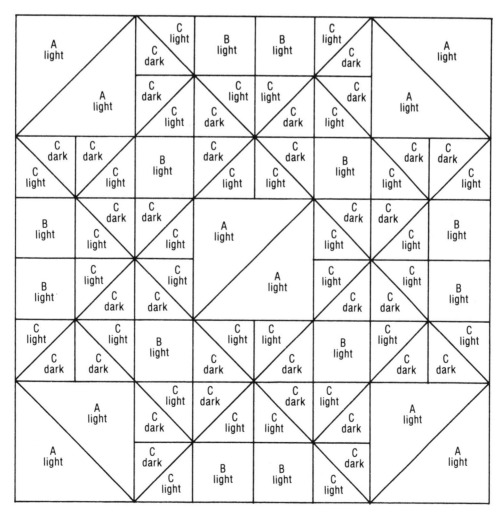

Octagonal Star

Use this 16″ block in a sampler quilt, or make 30 blocks and set them five across and six down with a 3″ border made of the medium fabric, to create an 86″ × 102″ quilt top.

Fabric requirements for quilt top

Light fabric	6¾ yds
Medium fabric	3½ yds
Dark fabric	4½ yds

Number of pieces to be cut

	for block	for quilt top
Template A	4 light	120 light
Template B	4 light	120 light
Template B	4 medium	120 medium
Template B	12 dark	360 dark
Template C	40 light	1200 light
Template C	8 medium	240 medium
Template C	24 dark	720 dark
Border strips, 3½″ × 86½″		2 medium fabric
Border strips, 3½″ × 96½″		2 medium fabric

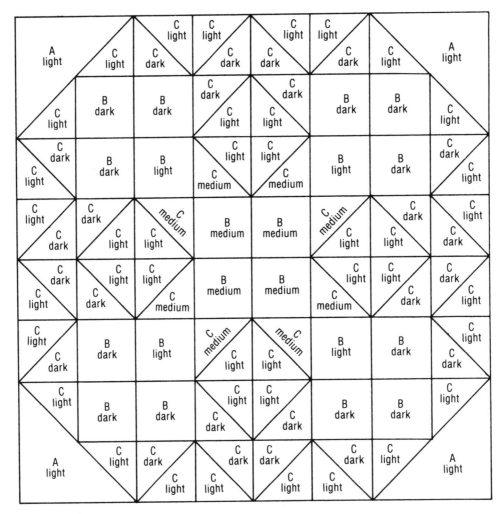

Odd-Fellows Star

Use this 16″ block in a sampler quilt, or make 30 blocks and set them five across and six down with a 3″ border made of the medium fabric, to create an 86″ × 102″ quilt top.

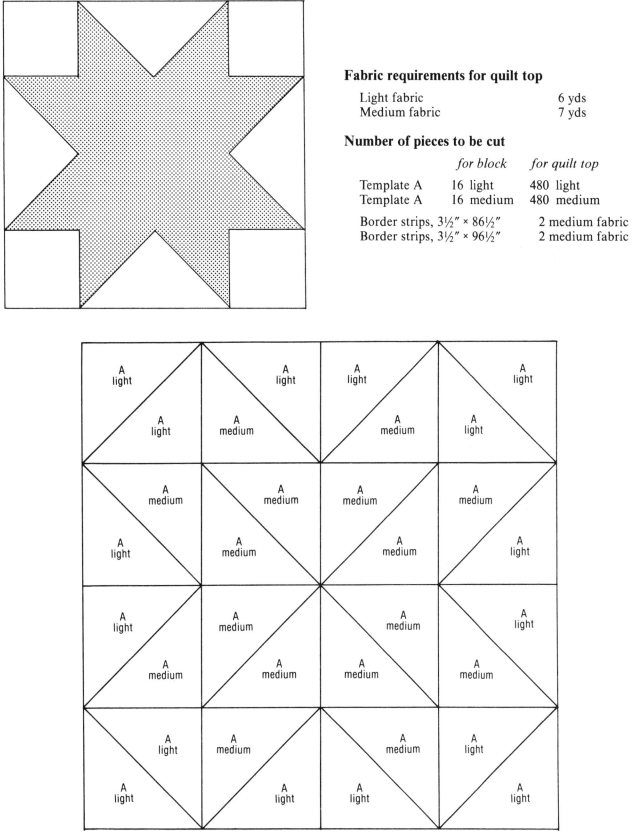

Fabric requirements for quilt top

Light fabric	6 yds
Medium fabric	7 yds

Number of pieces to be cut

	for block	*for quilt top*
Template A	16 light	480 light
Template A	16 medium	480 medium
Border strips, 3½″ × 86½″		2 medium fabric
Border strips, 3½″ × 96½″		2 medium fabric

Patriotic Star

Use this 16″ block in a sampler quilt, or make 30 blocks and set them five across and six down with a 3″ border made of the medium fabric, to create an 86″ × 102″ quilt top.

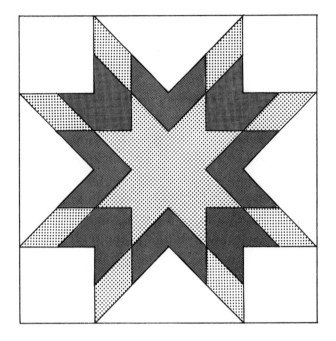

Fabric requirements for quilt top

Light fabric (white)	6 yds
Medium fabric (red)	4½ yds
Dark fabric (blue)	3¾ yds

Number of pieces to be cut

	for block	for quilt top
Template A	16 light	480 light
Template E	8 medium	240 medium
Template E (reversed)	8 medium	240 dark
Template E	8 dark	240 dark
Template E (reversed)	8 dark	240 dark
Border strips, 3½″ × 86½″	2 medium fabric	
Border strips, 3½″ × 96½″	2 medium fabric	

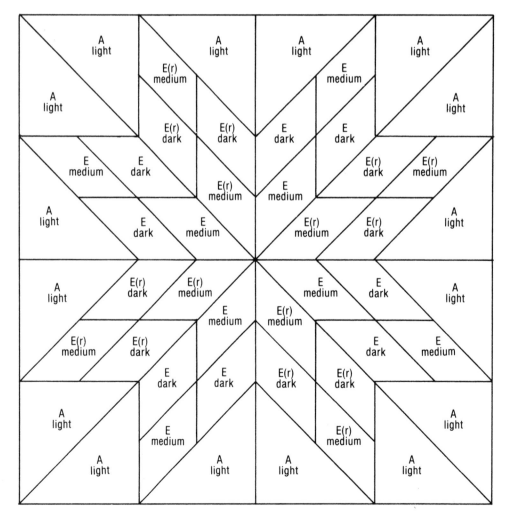

Pieced Star

Use this 16″ block in a sampler quilt, or make 30 blocks and set them five across and six down with a 3″ border made of the dark fabric, to create an 86″ × 102″ quilt top.

Fabric requirements for quilt top

Light fabric	6 yds
Dark fabric	7 yds

Number of pieces to be cut

	for block	*for quilt top*
Template A	16 light	480 light
Template A	16 dark	480 dark
Border strips, 3½″ × 86½″		2 dark fabric
Border strips, 3½″ × 96½″		2 dark fabric

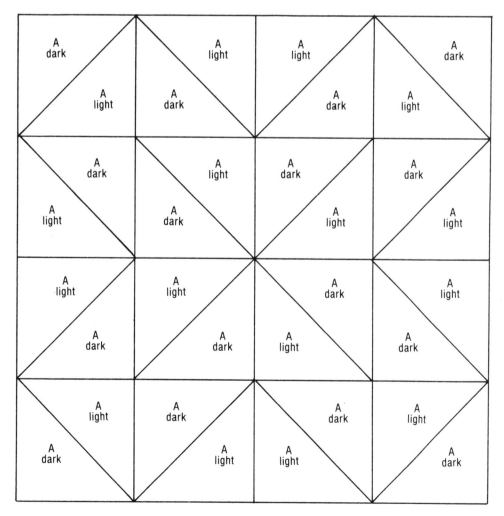

Pinwheel Star

Use this 16″ block in a sampler quilt, or make 30 blocks and set them five across and six down with a 3″ border made of the dark fabric, to create an 86″ × 102″ quilt top.

Fabric requirements for quilt top

Light fabric	9¼ yds
Dark fabric	5¼ yds

Number of pieces to be cut

	for block	for quilt top
Template A	20 light	600 light
Template C	12 light	360 light
Template C	36 dark	1080 dark
Border strips, 3½″ × 86½″		2 dark fabric
Border strips, 3½″ × 96½″		2 dark fabric

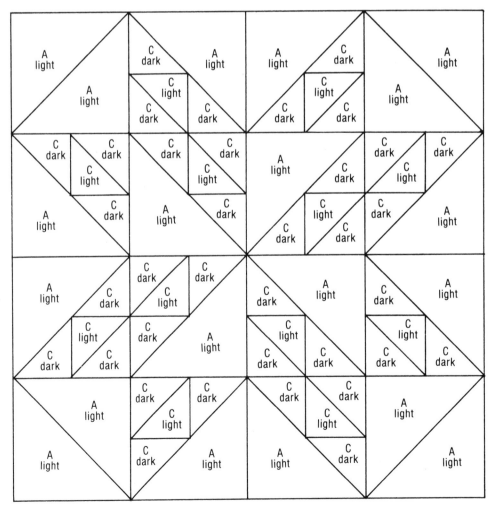

Ring Around the Star

Use this 16″ block in a sampler quilt, or make 30 blocks and set them five across and six down with a 3″ border made of the medium fabric, to create an 86″ × 102″ quilt top.

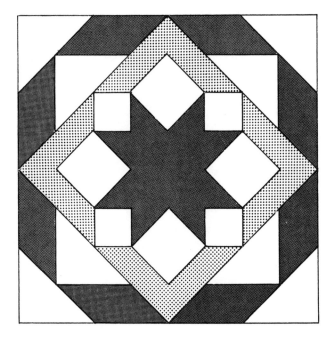

Fabric requirements for quilt top

Light fabric	5½ yds
Medium fabric	4 yds
Dark fabric	4½ yds

Number of pieces to be cut

	for block	for quilt top
Template A	8 light	240 light
Template B	4 light	120 light
Template B	12 dark	360 dark
Template C	16 light	480 light
Template C	24 medium	720 medium
Template C	24 dark	720 dark
Border strips, 3½″ × 86½″		2 medium fabric
Border strips, 3½″ × 96½″		2 medium fabric

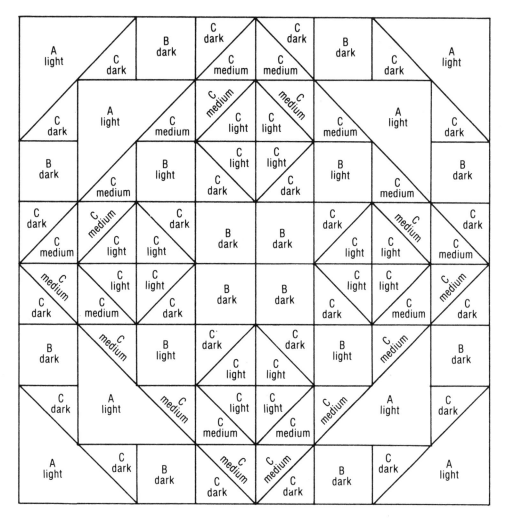

Royal Star

Use this 16″ block in a sampler quilt, or make 30 blocks and set them five across and six down with a 3″ border made of the dark fabric, to create an 86″ × 102″ quilt top.

Fabric requirements for quilt top

Light fabric	6½ yds
Dark fabric	7½ yds

Number of pieces to be cut

	for block	for quilt top
Template A	12 light	360 light
Template A	12 dark	360 dark
Template C	16 light	480 light
Template C	16 dark	480 dark
Border strips, 3½″ × 86½″		2 dark fabric
Border strips, 3½″ × 96½″		2 dark fabric

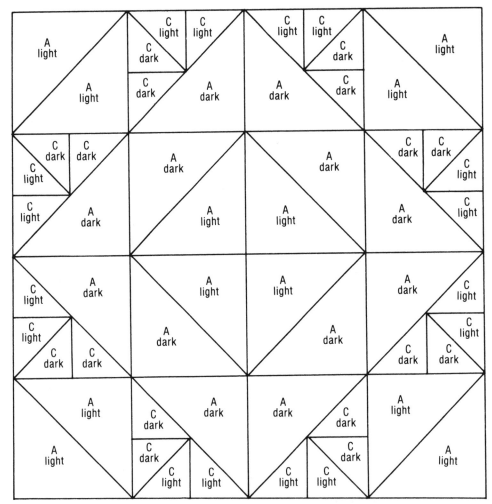

Star and Chains

Use this 16″ block in a sampler quilt, or make 30 blocks and set them five across and six down with a 3″ border made of the medium fabric, to create an 86″ × 102″ quilt top.

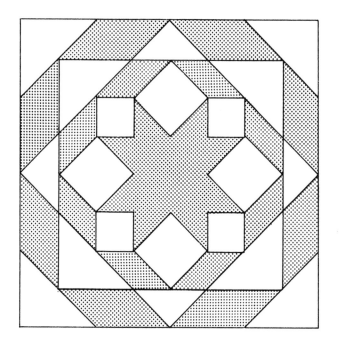

Fabric requirements for quilt top

Light fabric	6½ yds
Medium fabric	7¼ yds

Number of pieces to be cut

	for block	for quilt top
Template A	8 light	240 light
Template B	4 light	120 light
Template B	12 medium	360 medium
Template C	24 light	720 light
Template C	40 medium	1200 medium
Border strips, 3½″ × 86½″		2 medium fabric
Border strips, 3½″ × 96½″		2 medium fabric

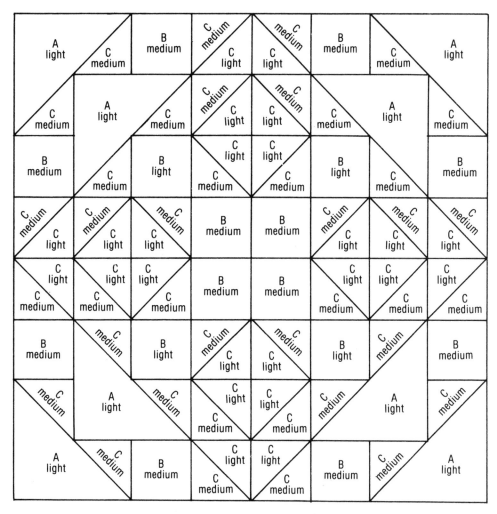

Starry Path

Use this 16″ block in a sampler quilt, or make 30 blocks and set them five across and six down with a 3″ border made of the dark fabric, to create an 86″ × 102″ quilt top.

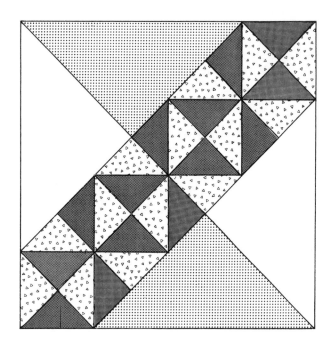

Fabric requirements for quilt top

Light fabric	3½ yds
Bright fabric	3½ yds
Medium fabric	3½ yds
Dark fabric	4 yds

Number of pieces to be cut

	for block	*for quilt top*
Template A	8 light	240 light
Template A	8 medium	240 medium
Template C	4 light	120 light
Template C	28 bright	840 bright
Template C	4 medium	120 medium
Template C	28 dark	840 dark
Border strips, 3½″ × 86½″		2 dark fabric
Border strips, 3½″ × 96½″		2 dark fabric

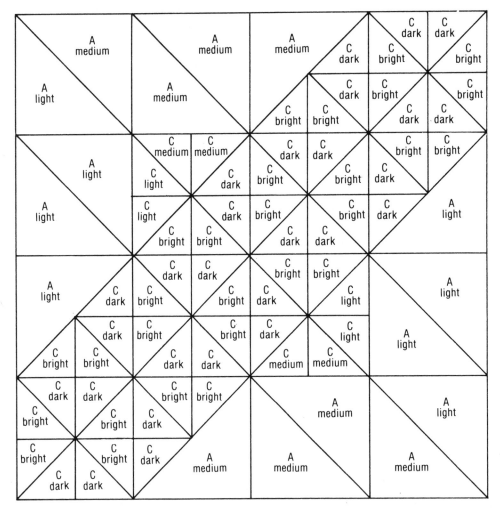

Stars and Squares

Use this 16″ block in a sampler quilt, or make 30 blocks and set them five across and six down with a 3″ border made of the dark fabric, to create an 86″ × 102″ quilt top.

Fabric requirements for quilt top

Light fabric	7½ yds
Dark fabric	5½ yds

Number of pieces to be cut

	for block	for quilt top
Template A	16 light	480 light
Template A	8 dark	240 dark
Template B	4 light	120 light
Template B	4 dark	120 dark
Template C	8 light	240 light
Template C	8 dark	240 dark
Border strips, 3½″ × 86½″		2 dark fabric
Border strips, 3½″ × 96½″		2 dark fabric

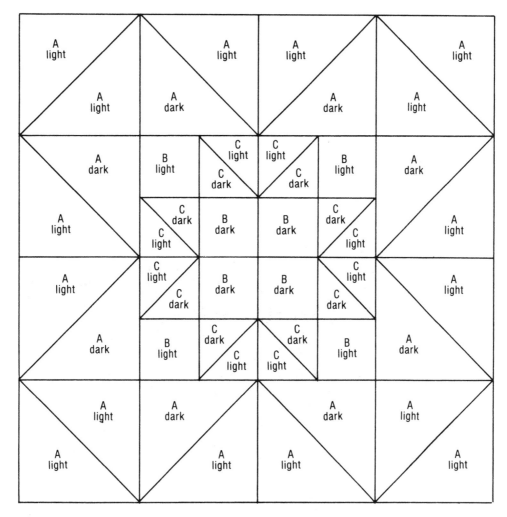

Trailing Star

Use this 16″ block in a sampler quilt, or make 30 blocks and set them five across and six down with a 3″ border made of the dark fabric, to create an 86″ × 102″ quilt top.

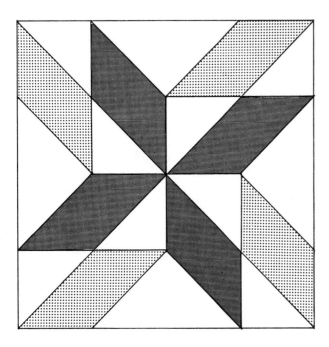

Fabric requirements for quilt top

Light fabric	6 yds
Medium fabric	3 yds
Dark fabric	4 yds

Number of pieces to be cut

		for block	for quilt top
Template A	16 light		480 light
Template A	8 medium		240 medium
Template A	8 dark		240 dark
Border strips, 3½″ × 86½″			2 dark fabric
Border strips, 3½″ × 96½″			2 dark fabric

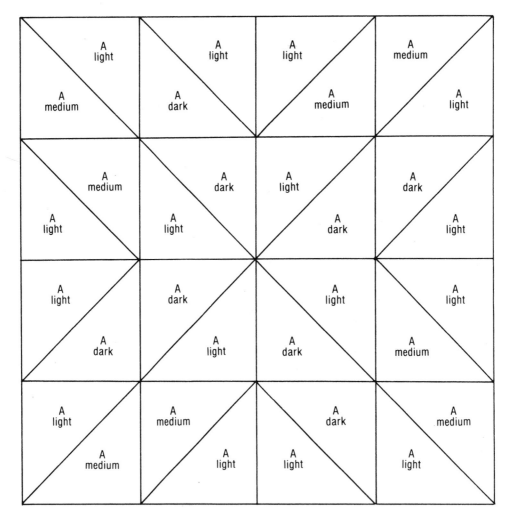